PRAISE ABOUT EVOLVED ADVISOR

"Patrick is leading from the front as an entrepreneur, thought leader and financial caregiver. His uncanny ability to educate and inspire his students and those around him combined with his servant's heart, ensure he's leaving the world a better place. I believe in challenging the status quo and teaching my clients how to live their best lives all while sitting on the same side of the table as them. Patrick has been able to lay out a road map for me on how to build the practice and business I knew I wanted. I have found my tribe with Patrick and his team of amazing badasses!"

- JESSE TODISCO
ADVISOR, AUTHOR, SPEAKER

"Patrick is helping to change the financial services industry as we know it. Patrick provided me with clarity and instilled confidence in my abilities necessary to be a better financial caregiver, trusted advisor, and entrepreneur. Patrick's clear, concise, and actionable guidance was easy to integrate into my business, resulting in more effective marketing, additional sales, and increased the productivity in my overall business. Working with Patrick has fast tracked my business and allowed me to live the entrepreneurial life on my terms, all while taking care of clients."

- ANTHONY REYNOLDS

ADVISOR

"Patrick Tucker is a revelation. This book is a gift. It's full of tools, guidance, and lessons. If you read it once, you'll gift it a dozen times."

- ANDREW NAUENBURG

SPEAKER, WRITER, ENTREPRENEUR, FOUNDER OF PONDER PROJECT

"A transformational and visionary roadmap for the entrepreneurial advisor. Patrick offers simple but invaluable advice on how to be successful in the financial services industry without compromising your morals."

-ANDREW WOLFE

FOUNDER OF VIRCHEW

THE
EVOLVED
ADVISOR

TRUE MEASURE
FINANCIAL ADVISORS

PATRICK TUCKER

THE
ΞVOLVΞD
ADVISOR

BREAK AWAY AND DESIGN AN ADVISORY BUSINESS AROUND YOUR LIFESTYLE

TRUE MEASURE
FINANCIAL ADVISORS

Published by: Throne Publishing Group
Cover and Layout Design: Amy Gehling
Proofer: Amy Rollinger

Throne Publishing Group
2329 N Career Ave #215
Sioux Falls, SD 57107

www.ThronePG.com

DEDICATION

This is dedicated to those who throughout my life's journey have helped instill my love of learning. My parents, teachers, mentors, my amazing team and most importantly my partner in life, my wife Sue.

TABLE OF CONTENTS

INTRODUCTION

INTRODUCTION

Money affects everyone. Whether you have a lot or very little, so much of our lives depend on money. This, however, offers a great opportunity for ourselves and for our clients. There are not many careers or business opportunities out there that impact people's daily lives to such a great extent.

As a financial planner, I get to influence lives. If you are my client, and I guide you well through your financial lifetime, I could endow you and your family—and maybe even your grandchildren—with greater choices and opportunities. This amazing type of work means everything to me. It is an honor to be involved in empowering families in these decisions, opening up greater possibilities in their future lives. I truly love what I do.

Years ago, I used to be licensed as a broker and an insurance agent, receiving most of my compensation in the form of commissions, and I wasn't happy. Working for larger firms was all about selling and producing, but that wasn't why I got into financial planning. I got into this great business because I wanted to advise people and guide them well through their financial needs. So I left the firms and started my own.

Today, I am an advice-based planner running a seven-figure, recurring revenue business, and I want to teach you how to be an entrepreneur and start your own business in the financial advisory field.

I want to show you how to be a good advisor and how to understand and relate to the human person. I want to encourage you and mentor you toward entrepreneurial freedom because I know it well, and I believe in it. If you have the desire to leave a large firm and become a self-employed financial advisor, I want you to win.

The best part about all of this is that I am in the trenches with you now. As my business continues to grow, I'm living what I'm teaching, which means I'm learning, too! I'm constantly adapting to the changing needs of my clients, and, as an advice-based planner who focuses on relationships, you can, too.

You can positively influence the financial outcomes for families and generations to come. What a great honor! Let's get started.

PART ONE

STARTING A BUSINESS

CHAPTER ONE

WHAT IS ADVICE-BASED PLANNING?

CHAPTER ONE

WHAT IS ADVICE-BASED PLANNING?

If you have had any experience in financial advising, you've likely been exposed to multiple methods of doing business. Most advisors who work for larger firms use the brokerage model, which involves advisors making a commission off any product they sell. This is one of the reasons why advisors are falsely represented as "salespeople" and why many of them are not trusted by their clients.

In the financial world, there is absolutely a better way to serve people.

However, before we spend the rest of this book talking about advice-based planning, I want to clarify for you the differences among commission-based, fee-based and fee-only advising models. If you want to run a business in the financial world, it's important that this makes sense to you because only then can you best serve your clients as a genuine, trustworthy and authentic advisor—nothing more, nothing less.

Commission-based planner: A commission-based planner only gets paid on commission. At the big firms, the predominant mover of revenue is commission, particularly if the advisor sells life insurance-based products. This area is where I believe the most abuse is happening in our industry because the salesmanship will take whatever form it needs to for the advisor to make money.

Fee-based planner: This term stresses out the industry so much that both the client and the advisor can get confused. Even the language is scattered—they might be financial planners, financial advisors, wealth managers, stockbrokers or fund experts. So much noise! But this term simply means that the advisor has licenses to both charge the client a commission and to charge a fee—such as financial planning fees, project fees, or investment management fees,—for the oversight and management of client portfolios. The advisor has the choice to do either, but the problem here is that the advisor still may be heavily influenced in choosing what is best for the advisor. There is little stake in what is best for the client.

For example, if a client has a portfolio valued at $1 million, the advisor may put him in a portfolio at, say, Merrill Lynch, and then charge the client whatever Merrill Lynch tells him to charge. Then the revenue would come into the firm and the advisor would get his chunk— whatever percentage that may be. But because the advisor also has his life insurance licenses, he can also get paid a lot of commission on an insurance sale on top of the percentage Merrill Lynch is giving him for the $1 million portfolio management. As you see, fee-based planners get to choose multiple forms by which they get paid.

Hybrid: In between a fee-based and a fee-only planner is a hybrid, which means the advisor has his own RIA (Registered Investment Advisor) but keeps some of his licensing as a broker dealer so he can still sell commissioned products like insurance, annuities, or MLPs. Even though hybrid advisors use both the commission and fee-based structures in their business, it is a step toward independence. Some people may need to be a hybrid advisor until they can move enough clients toward a recurring revenue model and no longer need any commission work for their income.

Fee-only planner: A fee-only planner does not receive any commission. The advisor drops all registered representative and insurance licenses, except the Series 65 or 66, which lawfully allows one to give advice as a fiduciary and charge fees. Even though this advisor is generally more respectful of the client's best interest, the term is unfortunately branded and marketed to the consumer in a way that highlights compensation.

Advice-Based Planner: Lastly, we have an advice-based planner (hey, that's me!), which is also a fee-only planner—they are one and the same—however, advice-based planners market themselves as advisors, not by how they are compensated. An advice-based planner charges clients as a fee-only advisor but operates as an advice-based business.

An advice-based planner is about the business of advice. We are in this book together right now because I want to teach you the craft of advising, not the craft of describing compensation.

Even though I am a fee-only advisor and do not receive any commission, I choose to use the term advice-based advisor instead because it is a better description of what we as an industry should actually be doing. This, however, is not the industry standard. As you can see in the above model descriptions, the industry, unfortunately, wants to describe itself by however it makes money, and that just doesn't feel right to me. Let's instead serve our clients and represent our business as the advice givers we desire to be in the first place.

In an advice-based model, the advisor is paid for quality guidance, which includes the time they spend meeting with clients, researching proper financial channels for each client, and making recommendations on financial decisions. Advisors are paid a flat fee, regardless of how many or what type of financial products they sell. Those who use an advice-based model can bill for hourly consulting, charge flat planning fees, charge a monthly subscription rate, or charge their clients based on assets under management. However you choose to bill is based on your unique situation and the type of clients you have.

Now, some advisors who leave a large firm to start their own advice-based business find that starting with a hybrid model helps ease transition. Because they can continue to work with a broker dealer, they have help with the administration and operations that might otherwise feel overwhelming once out on their own. A hybrid model allows administration support as the advisor transitions to advice-based business ownership.

An advice-based structure is truly the best way to provide value to clients while maintaining integrity as you grow a seven-figure business. I've been using this structure since I started True Measure and have found it to be a highly successful one. If you want to start your own financial planning business, I would advise you to do the same. Let me show you some benefits of utilizing the advice-based model to build a successful business.

ADVANTAGES OF ADVICE-BASED PLANNING

No more "hamster wheel": Anyone who has been in commissioned sales knows how frustrating the "hamster wheel" can be. You make sales only to find that your quotas continually increase, and you have to generate more and more sales just to keep your head above water. It's exhausting, and not healthy for you or your clients. When you run an advice-based model, the constant stress to produce more sales goes away.

More trust: It's difficult for a client to truly trust you when they know you're making a commission off every product you sell to them. However, when clients pay a flat fee for financial advice, they no longer view every recommendation with a skeptical eye. They know you have their best interest at heart and will advise them to make choices that benefit them—not your own bank account. You become less of a salesperson and more of a mentor to each of your clients.

Focus on value: The brokerage model sets up advisors to focus on sales first. Value actually comes secondary—if even at all—so most brokerage-model advisors consistently have their eyes on their quota. When you are advice-based, your focus becomes how happy your clients are with your advice and guidance. Advice-based planners can also focus on personality assessments or behavior models to enhance value with clients.

Advice-based planners focus on the valuable advice they can provide for each client. Therefore, they actually select the clients they choose to work with. Sometimes certain clients may not be the best fit for your advice-based business. An advisor may have a client who doesn't appreciate or need financial counsel, or they might not be able to afford your monthly fees. You may have a client who is retired and no longer in need of active planning services or you may have clients who make a large number of trades in a short amount of time. For you to be able to provide real value to clients, you will need to make sure the working relationship is a positive fit for both you and your client.

Also, an advisor may need to set boundaries, and this can be difficult for new advice-based advisors. A commission-based structure has limits built in—i.e., the more a client trades, the more they pay their advisor—whereas an advice-based model has no limits to what a client does under an advisor's flat fee. Fortunately, with your intent to build honest, genuine relationships with your clients, these conversations are best discussed upfront to ensure a positive outcome for both you and your client.

CHANGE YOUR MINDSET

If you've been in the industry for a while and are used to a commission-based structure, it might take a little time to change the way you adapt to an advice-based structure. That's okay! Nothing worth doing well happens overnight, but the key is to slowly work your mindset toward thinking more and more like an entrepreneur and business owner. Here are suggestions to inspire you along the way.

Read books: As a lifelong learner, I always make time in my day for reading, and I suggest this to anyone who wants to build an entrepreneurial business. Many people say they don't have time to read, but this just isn't true. They just haven't made time in their day to read.

Think about your day. Are you really spending all your waking hours doing something that cannot be replaced by a half hour of reading? Most people waste hours a day watching mindless television, playing video games, or on commutes where they do nothing but stare out the window or at their phone. If you truly don't have any wasted time during your day, it is worth it to wake up a half hour earlier to get some reading in. Yes, it's that important.

I have gained a lot of knowledge from the hundreds of books I read each year and am always excited to recommend my favorites to others. When it comes to changing your mindset to that of an advice-based planner, here are books I most often recommend.

- Mindset by Carol Dweck
- Drive: The Surprising Truth About What Motivates Us by Daniel Pink
- Switch: How to Change Things When Change is Hard by Chip and Dan Heath
- The One Thing: The Surprisingly Simple Truth Behind Extraordinary Results by Gary Keller and Jay Papasan
- Quiet: The Power of Introverts in a World That Can't Stop Talking by Susan Cain (this one is perfect for entrepreneurs who think they can't start their own business because they aren't extroverted

enough)

- Screw It, Let's Do It: Lessons in Life by Richard Branson
- Tools of Titans by Tim Ferriss

Take an entrepreneurial advisor course: Do you have what it takes to be an entrepreneurial advice-based planner? I think you do, but there are also courses available developed specifically to help you change your mindset and the course of your business. Our course at True Measure, The Evolved Financial Advisor, offers videos, workbooks, and resources to help you make the change. You do not need to go on this journey alone!

Talk to others who have made the change: More and more advisors today are making the switch to an advice-based entrepreneurial business. You should not view these other advisors as competition—they are sources of information, guidance and inspiration. I believe that mentors are a key aspect to a financial planner's success and suggest you have a number of them whom you meet with regularly.

You might also want to join a forum or online community with others who are starting their own advice-based planning business. For example, we offer a closed mastermind Facebook group for those who take The Evolved Financial Advisor course, so they can discuss ideas and challenges, and support each other on their journeys.

The financial planning industry need not be competitive; we could be a community supporting one another!

HISTORY OF ADVICE-BASED PLANNING

In the 1960s, financial planning services were primarily inter-changeable with insurance sales. Brokers had all the information, control, and power. Anyone who wanted access to investing had to go through a broker. Then, in 1969, a meeting of twelve men in a Chicago hotel room began to change all that. They set out to create a new profession within the financial industry that was based on consulting rather than salesmanship.

That meeting was the birthplace of our financial planning industry today. Not only did it establish the professional code of ethics we abide by, this convening also established the education and experience needed to become a financial advisor.

Over the next half decade, the industry continued to evolve and in 1983 established The National Association of Personal Financial Advisors (NAPFA), from which emerged the fee-only planner. Although we saw advice-based planners as early as the 1980s, this area of the industry really picked up steam in the 1990's and early 2000's with the rise of technology and the internet. Soon, there were all kinds of ways for people to buy products, and those products become cheaper and more accessible than ever. With so much information people were suddenly either too afraid to invest or too overwhelmed by financial intelligence in general. This has increased the need for valuable and trustworthy advising planners to help clients think through it all.

Unlike at the beginning of financial planning years ago, advice-based planning today is much more transparent, an approach that enlightens and empowers clients to make the best decisions for themselves. When I started in the industry twenty years ago, it seemed like people were touting advisory planning. I even excitedly joined a firm that was talking about advising, but when I got there, they weren't actually advising. They were just selling products and disguising it as advice.

In advice-based planning, there are no disguises—just honesty, guidance and genuine relationship.

Whether you just earned your MBA or have been working for a broker for twenty years, you can become an advice-based business owner, and you can start today. No matter where you are in your career, I am here to empower and equip you to start your own business and succeed.

CHAPTER TWO

LEAVING THE FIRM

CHAPTER TWO

LEAVING THE FIRM

If you are at a large firm now, there are steps you need to take before leaving to start your own business. And don't leave too soon! Maximize your time there, and be patient with yourself as you lay new groundwork and build relationships. Here are steps to follow.

Identify other advisors who may be leaving the business: Take a look around your firm. Who else do you think is ready to leave? Look both for those advisors who are near retirement as well as those who are getting out of financial planning and looking for employment in other fields. These advisors present a golden opportunity for you as they will need someone to take over their book of business once they leave.

Review your employee contract with an employment attorney: What paperwork did you sign when you joined the firm you are currently with? Meet with an employment attorney to go over any documents you may have signed and identify any issues you may run into when leaving the firm. Some firms will have their advisors sign non-disclosures or non-competes. Depending on the actual wording of the documents, they may or may not present a potential problem, but a skilled employment attorney will pinpoint red flags.

Build relationships: There are important professional relationships that can seamlessly transfer to your new business and help you build clientele. These might include:

CPAs: If you have not already built a relationship with a CPA, now is the time. CPAs are excellent sources of referrals as most of their clients also need financial planning services.

Possible partners: Are there other planners in your firm who you think would be a good fit to join your business down the road? If you have not already done so, put in some time and effort to get to know them better.

Clients: After you leave a firm, you cannot approach your clients to pursue continued business with them because the firm could sue you. This is why you want to consult a contract attorney to review your employment contract. Instead, let your clients know of your plans before you depart and leave them with your new contact information should they choose to continue business with you. They may even refer their friends and family to you. Concentrate on those clients who are open to advice and are not transactional focused, and be sure you haven't put these types of clients into financial products or portfolios that lock them into your current firm.

Mentors: I've said this before, and I'll say it again. You can never have enough mentors! I think you should nurture and develop anywhere from four to twenty good mentors, and each of them should be ten to twenty years ahead of you in the business. Don't limit yourself to people in the financial industry, either. Your ideal mentor network will be a combination of those who have worked in corporate finance, those who have established an independent advisor firm, and a few individuals in different industries altogether.

Each mentor alone could save you one to three years of learning—along with avoiding mistakes and frustration. This could easily mean a ten-year acceleration in your business! When you view it this way, the time commitment is well worth it, right? And this is easy to do before you go out on your own.

Cultivate your network by meeting with others in the industry and asking who they think you should talk to. Look through your LinkedIn connections and see who fits your criteria. When you reach out to these individuals, you might be surprised at how receptive they are to meeting. If they aren't, don't take it personally. They may not be in the right place to offer this type of guidance right now.

These relationships can take years to form, so you should start as soon as possible. You can't rush them. Some of my most treasured mentors didn't share the really good stuff with me until we'd been meeting for over two years. But believe me when I say... it was worth the wait.

Take advantage of extra learning opportunities offered by the firm: Does your firm offer compensation for taking continuing education courses? Or do they offer other perks such as in-house trainings? Whatever opportunities there are for extra learning, take them.

Some advisors shy away from doing this because they feel they are taking advantage of their current employer. Once they have made the decision to leave, they feel they should not benefit any longer from what the firm makes available to them. I simply don't believe that's true. If you are not taking every opportunity available to you to learn more and expand your knowledge, you are doing a disservice to your clients, plain and simple. You are not being deceptive or manipulative to the firm where you currently work. You are simply growing your career, as any firm would hope you are striving to do.

LICENSES

Even if you are new to the industry and do not have a firm to leave, you still need to be cultivating relationships with CPAs and mentors as soon as possible. If self-employment is the end goal, then begin taking strides immediately to get there, no matter how long the process actually takes!

When someone wants to enter the great world of investment professionals, they must first pass qualification exams and receive certain licenses. Now if you are preparing to leave a firm, you may already have all the exams or licenses you need to go out on your own. It just depends on the environment you've been working in thus far and what continuing education you've gone through.

If you want to work in the advice-based business, you need to complete and pass the Series 65 exam, an exam that qualifies you to provide investment advice, retirement planning, portfolio management strategies and fiduciary advice to clients. This license allows you to charge fees for providing investment advice.

The exam you need to register for to get your Series 65 license is called the Uniform Investment Advisor Law Examination, and it is administered by FINRA. Once you register for the exam, you have 120 days to complete it. If you don't pass, you need to wait thirty days to take it again. If you fail three times, then you need to wait 180 days before you can re-test, but you can take the test as many times as you need to pass.

To study for the exam, we suggest taking our "Fast Track" course at True Measure, which offers study guides, online practice quizzes and Facebook study groups. It's imperative that you identify your learning style and how you best prepare for exams.

Other FINRA exams or ways to qualify as an advice-based advisor include passing the Series 66 exam, which qualifies you as both a securities agent and an investment advisor. Professional designations such as the Certified Financial Planner (CFP), the Chartered Financial Analyst (CFA) or the Certified Public Accountant (CPA) also may satisfy the regulatory bodies and designate you as an investment advisor representative (IAR).

Whether you are leaving a firm or starting fresh, take time to prepare and study for whichever licenses you need, and use those mentoring relationships to help you talk through any confusion. You've got this!

CHAPTER THREE

CHOOSING YOUR WORKSPACE

CHAPTER THREE

CHOOSING YOUR WORKSPACE

Are you starting to look and feel like a business owner yet? You've got your licenses, your mentors, and your growing relationships to help you start your own advice based business, but when you close your eyes and picture yourself as a successful business owner, what does your office environment look like? How does it make you feel?

Like a rock star, I hope.

If you were once employed at a firm, you likely sat in a stuffy office space, suppressing your creativity and leaving you every day feeling stressed, over-worked and unfulfilled. Let's change that!

One of the best parts about starting your own business is that you get to customize it. You can choose what works best for you and your clients, and you can craft an environment that feels productive, comfortable and empowering for you.

Unfortunately, much of society has painted a picture of

financial planners as stuffy businesspeople in formal suits and working in wood-paneled offices on the top floor of high-rise buildings. With this in mind, does it surprise you that people are intimidated to talk to their financial planners?

Fortunately, the face of the financial planning industry is changing for the better every day, and advisors have the freedom to establish a unique working environment where both they and their clients feel comfortable to talk, brainstorm and learn. Consider these work environments:

Formal office: Many financial advisors enjoy having a formal office to go to every day. I admit, there is something comforting about a secure office where you can welcome clients to talk about important financial matters. It is nice to have a traditional office setting with a receptionist, a conference room, and amenities that make both you and your clients feel comfortable. You can also personalize it and make it your own. Let your personality shine in the artwork, the furniture, and the location. Just have conviction that this is what you want and not what you think is expected of you as a financial planner. It's not.

Casual office: Many advisors, however, prefer a more casual environment. If you are younger or have younger clients, this setting is preferable. This can include a co-working office space where colleagues rent desks and share a receptionist and conference rooms.

Whichever you choose, take time to explore areas and buildings in your community available for rent, and don't settle until the space speaks to your vision!

Work from home: Many advisors love the freedom of being able to work from home. They can take their kids to school or simply have the flexibility to not commute to the office every day. Others, however, find it difficult to focus amid their living space, where there is always laundry or dishes to tend to. They can never fully get into a work groove and end up being less productive. Working from home might also mean you have to meet clients in a public place that lacks privacy.

Here are some additional thoughts on working from home. Make sure you can focus in that environment. Most of those I know who work successfully from home have a designated "office" where they can close the door and concentrate. This also helps to differentiate between work and family, and gives them space to keep safe their documents, client information, and computer.

Second, ensure you have a good place to meet clients. Maybe there is a coffee shop nearby that has a private meeting room you can reserve. Or, perhaps, one of your friends has an office with a conference room that you might use as needed.

Finally, be honest with yourself. You might think working from home is the best of both worlds; but remember you didn't start your own business so you could sleep in until ten and lounge in your pajamas all day. You started a business so you could create the life you want, in a fulfilling career, that has the capacity to impact generations. So, make it happen, and be sure your work environment is empowering, not distracting.

Work virtually: Technology has advanced to the point where you really can work from anywhere, which means you don't need an office at all. Virtual hangouts are ideal for those who enjoy travel or who have clients scattered throughout the country. With an internet connection and a laptop, or other mobile device, you essentially have everything you need to run your business.

If you choose to work or meet clients remotely, consider cloud-based video conferencing tools or Google Hangouts, a communication platform with both video and messaging. You can also conduct video chats on social media, and there are document-sharing options online to help you work with clients.

Now close your eyes again and picture yourself as a successful advice-based business owner. I hope that environmental vision is a little clearer!

CHAPTER FOUR

ESTABLISHING YOUR BUSINESS

CHAPTER FOUR

ESTABLISHING YOUR BUSINESS

The practicalities of starting a business can seem overwhelming, especially if you've spent most of your working life in a corporation or other large business where all details were taken care of for you. Don't let this deter you, though. Setting up your business is not as complicated as you might think. The most important part of this process is to practice good risk management and work with a good CPA and business attorney who have experience in the finance industry and helping entrepreneurs. The rest will run smoothly! Let's break it down.

Choose a business structure: Do you want to be a sole proprietor, LLC, or corporation? The type you choose depends on your plans for the business, how many people will be involved on the ownership level, and tax considerations. Meet with your CPA or business attorney to help you decide the correct business structure.

Pick and register your business name with the Secretary of State: Have you considered what you're going to name your business? Many financial entrepreneurs use their names when they go independent, and this is certainly an option. However, a good business name can help with branding your business, standing out in your field, and telling your clients what you are all about.

Once you decide, register your new business name with the Secretary of State. Be prepared with a couple of names, in case your first choice is already taken. Again, this is where a business attorney might come in handy. They can walk you through the registration process and answer any questions you may have along the way.

Obtain a federal tax ID number: A federal tax ID number is necessary for your new business. Fortunately, these are relatively quick and easy to obtain. Go to www.irs.gov and fill out your application. You should receive your ID number within six to eight weeks.

Open a business checking account: It's never a good idea to co-mingle funds when you own a business. Opening a business checking account is one of the first things you should do when you decide to go out on your own. Everything related to the business should go through this account, and you should keep good records of all your expenditures. This will help when it comes to tax time and will also help you develop a business budget. You may also want to consider getting a credit card for your business as this can help you keep track of expenditures and also qualify for rewards in the form of travel, gift cards, or cash back bonuses.

REGISTRATION FILING

To be an independent advisor, you must register your firm as a Registered Investment Advisor (RIA) and then register to be an IAR of the firm (Investment Advisory Representative). If you have been working for a financial firm, that firm will file a U5, which is the Uniform Termination Notice for Securities Industry Registration. This will then free you to file a U4, which is the Uniform Application for Securities Industry Registration or Transfer. You must fill out and register this form to become registered with a state securities regulator. Those who are new to the business need not worry about the U5 but will still need to file the U4.

To find the right forms and register them, you can use FINRA's IARD system, an electronic filing system that facilitates investment advisor registration. Use this system to process your application for becoming an RIA and file your U4. If you are registering with the SEC, you will pay their filing fees and be registered for the SEC. If you register at a state level, you will pay the state registration filing fees and be registered with the state.

INSURANCE NEEDS

When you open an independent business, you will need to take care of all the insurance needs of your office, for yourself and for any employees you take on. This is another area where working with a professional will be useful. Develop a relationship with a good commercial insurance representative (preferably one who has worked with others in the financial field), as he or she will ensure you are covered in all necessary areas. This includes property insurance, which covers losses to buildings and contents you own; general liability, which protects the business against third-party claims caused by negligence; workers compensation, which covers employees for job-related injuries or illness, as well as medical expenses, lost income, and rehabilitation expenses; bonds, which can reimburse for employee theft or embezzlement; and possible umbrella policies, which supplement existing coverages.

COMPLIANCE DOCUMENTS

Before you begin working with clients, you need to fill out the following compliance documents. Compliance is acting according to an order, a set of rules, or standard of law. These documents will need to be prepared prior to your RIA registration.

Form ADV Part 1: Form ADV is what investment advisors use to register with the Securities and Exchange Commission and state securities authorities. Part 1 requires you to fill out information about your business, including ownership, clients, employees, business practices, affiliations, and disciplinary events.

Form ADV Part 2A and 2B: Part 2 requires you to prepare understandable brochures about your advisory services, fee schedule, disciplinary information, educational and business background, and conflicts of interest to provide to your clients. Once filed, these will be available to the public.

Policies and procedure manual: This manual will help you make major decisions about your business and activities that you and your employees perform in your business. It will help you conduct day-to-day operations in a legal and uniform manner.

Privacy policy statement: This legal document discloses the way you will manage clients' data so their privacy is protected at all times.

Investment advisory contracts: State law requires that contracts between state-licensed investment advisors and their clients be in writing.

Code of ethics document: This outlines your mission statement and values, and how you plan to professionally approach problems based on your ethics, core values, and the standards of the profession.

Business continuity plan: This will spell out your process of creating a plan of prevention and/or recovery if there is a threat to your company.

COMPLIANCE SERVICE PROVIDERS

You can research and build your culture of compliance on your own, or you can hire a compliance services firm that will build it for you. We work with RIA in a Box, which frees us to do what we do best—advise clients! A compliance service will keep up with all the new compliance laws for you and package everything you need in a simplified format. By following their guidelines, you can have peace of mind that your business is compliant.

CHAPTER FIVE

CUSTODIAL RELATIONSHIPS

CHAPTER FIVE

CUSTODIAL RELATIONSHIPS

As a fully independent advice-based advisor, you will need to develop one or more custodial relationships so your clients' accounts remain secure.

A custodian is a financial institution that holds your clients' accounts in safekeeping. This includes their stocks, bonds, mutual funds, and any other investment type of account.

The purpose of using a custodian is to minimize risk. Custodians are large companies who are responsible for millions of dollars. They have security measures in place to minimize the risk of fraud, theft, or other losses, and have the technology and infrastructure in place to keep your clients' accounts safe. As an advisor, your value is in listening and guiding your clients; as a custodian, their value is in holding and keeping safe your clients' accounts.

When you work with a custodian, you are not turning your clients' money over to them. You are simply using their platform to execute the activities that are held in safekeeping for a client. Your clients will have access to their money just as they would in any other situation. Most record-keeping done by a custodian is now done electronically, although, some still offer the option of holding records in a physical form—such as in a stock certificate, if the client prefers.

CUSTODIAL RELATIONSHIP CHOICES

If you are just starting out, you will need to choose one or more custodians to hold your clients' accounts. In addition to researching custodians to see which is the best fit, you may also want to talk to mentors and others in the industry to see which custodians they have used.

If you've been in the industry for a while, it is likely you are familiar with one or more of these custodians. However, if you worked for a large firm, you likely held many of your accounts in-house. When you go fully independent, you will need all your accounts to be held with a custodian.

Choosing a custodian depends on how you wish to manage portfolios and how well the custodian aligns with your business. Consider how the custodian interfaces with the technology you use. The look and feel of the technology should match your ideal client experience. If your clients like to log in to the advisor sites you use, check out the custodian's technology from a client's perspective. Some custodians have the latest cutting-edge technology, while others offer third-party asset managers, which some advisors find helpful. Some have pre-built models you can use, while others have remarkably efficient and user-friendly websites that benefit both advisors and their clients.

Make your own choice based on research, personal preferences, and your way of doing business. By all means, talk to others in the industry about their experiences with different custodians. Regardless, have peace of mind knowing that all the custodians listed below are of the highest integrity and have stellar reputations. Your clients will be safe with any of them, so it really comes down to which custodian best fits your business.

TD Ameritrade
tdameritrade.com

Fidelity
fiws.fidelity.com

National Advisors Trust
nationaladvisorstrust.com

RBC Correspondent Services
rbc-as.com

Scottrade Advisor Services
advisor.scottrade.com

Trust Company of America
nationaladvisorstrust.com

CharlesSchwab Advisor Services
advisorservices.schwab.com

SEI
seic.com

NAVIGATING INVESTMENT MANAGEMENT

Once you have a custodial relationship in place, how are you as the advisor going to handle the investment and portfolio decisions? I encourage you here to focus more on the client and their behaviors and less on the technical, investment management side.

Your first option is to handle client portfolios via a custodian and act as the portfolio manager yourself. For example, if you established a custodial relationship with TD Ameritrade and opened a client account, you could design and build your own portfolios for your clients. With software and systems built into many of the custodial institutions, you can research, design, create any model you would like, and then apply it across all of your client accounts.

You also can use automated asset management programs, known as Robo platforms or Robo advisors. An example of this is Betterment, an investment company with inexpensive, index-tracking ETF models (exchange-traded funds). Betterment is efficient for both you and your client and is appropriate for smaller accounts or tech-savvy clients. Another automated management tool option is called Motif, which is essentially socialized portfolio management where models are created under different themes.

Lastly, you can outsource portfolio management using the chief investment officer model (CIO) or the turnkey asset management program (TAMP). The CIO model permits the advisor to manage the client portfolio on a discretionary basis and make changes in investments when needed, whereas the TAMP platform allows advisors to completely outsource the management of client assets. In a TAMP, you would not open a traditional custodial account with, say, TD Ameritrade; instead, you would go directly to a third-party asset management program, which acts as a custodial relationship and trust company.

Outsourcing investment management is efficient and the preferred method for most independent advisors because it allows you to focus on your value. When you outsource, you are like the general contractor, watching over the entire project while hiring specialists on behalf of your clients. You are doing your best to see that your clients are happy, and their assets are safe.

In financial service practices, everyone can run their business differently. Thus, our work can be both frustrating and fascinating because there are so many different avenues to explore! But take heed here and trust that even though custodial relationships and investment management options might feel overwhelming, you will find the right fit for your business and your advisory fashion. Put in the time and research to make informed choices as you move forward in building a successful business.

PART TWO

SUSTAINING A BUSINESS

CHAPTER SIX

TECHNOLOGY

CHAPTER SIX

TECHNOLOGY

Many advisors who go independent wonder about the proper
level of technology that they should incorporate into their
businesses. While it makes sense to maintain an authentic
relationship with clients, it is not practical to think you can run
a business today without being technologically savvy. Not only
can the right technology save you time and money, but it also
can make user experience more streamlined and interactive for
your clients.

However, if you pick the wrong technology, you could create
more hassle for yourself and those you work with. Know what
type of business you want to run before you purchase the new-
est gadgets and gizmos that may or may not work for you.

Much of your decision will be based on your office set-up,
personal preferences, and comfort level with different forms
of technology. Here are the basics you need to consider as you
prepare to handle clients efficiently and effectively.

COMPUTER HARDWARE

To run your advice-based advisor business successfully, you need reliable and user-friendly computer hardware. In many cases, connecting via email, Skype, or FaceTime will constitute the bulk of your communication with clients, especially if they are remote. The last thing you want is to drop calls, have trouble connecting, or find that your computer was infected with a virus and sent thousands of spam emails to everyone in your contact list. Put in the time and effort up front to be vigilant, so both your business and your clients can remain safe.

In most cases, you get what you pay for when it comes to technology. If you buy a bargain-basement laptop and pay your sister's kid to hook it up and install security software, you are asking for trouble! Instead, work with a professional who can help you make the right hardware decisions and ensure everything is hooked up and connected properly. These professionals are also a valuable resource down the road if you ever run into technical issues.

Here are examples of hardware pieces to consider for your business.

Desktop: If you prefer a larger computer screen and one hub, then a desktop might work well for you. A couple of my employees love their desktop Macs and swear by their efficiency. Some like the convenience of a laptop. I'm strictly an iPad person, as it allows me to do everything I need to do, and it is compact. However, this is simply a personal preference depending on how you work best.

Laptop: Does anyone exist without a laptop these days? If you have decided to work from home or have a more flexible office set-up, a laptop is usually best. The better quality laptops have almost all the capabilities of a desktop, and you can take them with you anywhere you go. Again, you get what you pay for here. Don't think you can get a refurbished five-year-old laptop for a steal and expect it to perform at a high level.

Tablet: Tablets are incredibly handy, especially if you travel a lot and meet clients at their office or in the field. A tablet is a portable personal computer with a touchscreen display instead of a keyboard. I recommend keeping one on you at all times. Even if you aren't using it for client meetings, you can still use it to read books, compile research, or perform other work while waiting in airports or in between meetings.

I use Apple products for my laptop, desktop, and tablets. Whether you choose Macs or PCs, it's important to remain consistent among all hardware. Not only do you want to learn how to work with them, you also want to ensure your products can be connected and work together optimally.

Printer: Yes, most records today can be kept digitally, but don't abandon a printer altogether. Many of your clients will still want physical copies of documents, and there are times when you'll need to send in paperwork. You don't need anything elaborate here. Just be sure your printer connects to your IT network and has scanning capabilities—and don't forget ink.

Apple TV: Apple TV was one of my best investments when I set up my office. These small, simple devices make it possible to wirelessly stream all of my iTunes content. This includes audiobooks, TV shows, videos, music, and more. It can connect to multiple Macs, also, so you can share it with co-workers or clients. I use my Apple TV in planning meetings and to display reports and concepts for my clients. We don't print client information or give clients any paper documents (unless requested), and this is because we use Apple TV to review information with them.

COMPUTER SOFTWARE

Below are examples of computer software that can make your job efficient, secure, and more profitable. I use all of these examples in my own business and find them each to be valuable.

Password vault: The golden rule of cyber security is to have strong, unique passwords. That means no using the same password twice, and no using obvious passwords that could be discovered by hackers. No doubt, this can be overwhelming, considering the average person has around 27 separate needs for passwords. The worst thing you can do is write down all your passwords in a notebook for your own benefit. What happens if you lose it? The best solution I have found is to use an online, secure password vault. Your passwords are always at your fingertips, and there is adequate security to keep them safe from cyber criminals.

Financial planning software: Using the right software here is key. You need a program that is easy for the client to understand while still providing a high level of functionality. Find software that you can quickly become familiar with, so you can use it to its best advantage.

Risk profiling software: The right risk profiling software will help both you and your clients better understand their portfolios and their tolerance for risk. This is a key component of knowing your clients on a deep level, to advise them to the best of your ability.

Bookkeeping software: Even if you work with an accountant (which I highly recommend), you will still want a reliable form of bookkeeping so you can track expenses, deductions, and other important bits of information to give your accountant when tax time arrives. Don't fall behind; stay on top of your bookkeeping.

Electronic document storage software: We deal with a lot of paperwork in this business. Even though it may be in digital form instead of endless stacks of paper, it still takes up room and can be tough to transport. Having online document storage makes it possible to keep the paperwork you need without hogging all your storage space on your computer. It also helps you get clients the documents they need without clogging their inbox.

Online meeting software: This is important for advisors who work remotely or have remote clients. There is only so much you can do via phone and email. At certain times, you need to see your clients or colleagues face-to-face. If it's not possible to physically be there, you can still visit with someone virtually via online meeting software.

However effectively you choose to use technology, consider the above guidance to ensure your business and office, no matter where it is located, are wired for success.

CHAPTER SEVEN

MARKETING

CHAPTER SEVEN

MARKETING

Initially, it may be a bit challenging for new entrepreneurs to bring in clients. If you're especially new to the financial business world, you have probably never had to drum up business before, and, if you've been working for a large firm, they probably did the majority of marketing for you. However, as we all know, you can't have a business without clients, so marketing and driving sales need to be an integral part of your business plan.

Whether you were able to bring with you a few clients from a previous firm or have zero clients in sight, you still have a new business to market. Here are several ideas to bring in the clients you need to be successful.

NETWORKING

Depending on your personality type and level of sociability, networking could be the most fun part of your job—or the part you dread the most. While extroverts tend to thrive on getting involved in multiple organizations and building new relationships, introverts shy away from "putting themselves out there" and often wonder if it is even necessary.

I do believe networking is important, but **how** you network is much more important than **if** you network. There is no single right way to get involved in the networking community. What may work well for someone else might not fit for you, so it is important to just get out there and get going. Consider these networking options:

Networking groups: Depending on what size of city you live in, there could be dozens or even hundreds of networking groups to join. These range from professional organizations to referral groups you attend weekly or monthly to meet other professionals with whom you can trade business.

Many financial planners flock to networking groups. This could mean that, at any given event, you could be in a room with a lot of your competition. So, unless you're willing to attend more functions and be of more value than any other planner in your community, these might be an inefficient use of your time.

There are, however, groups that limit their membership to one person in each profession. Seek and consider these, but, keep in mind, that you will be expected to attend a majority of the meetings and expected to drum up business for other members. Introverts actually tend to thrive in these groups because you get to know a core group of people instead of constantly having to meet and socialize with new individuals. If you're willing to put in the time and effort and get into a good one, these groups can be very profitable.

Referral partners: Referral partners don't necessarily have to be separate from networking groups. In fact, networking groups are great places to find ideal referral partners. In the financial industry, there are a number of professions you can look to for great referral partners who can pass you a lot of business (and vice versa). Here are a few examples of referral partners.

Divorce attorneys: When a couple gets divorced, one or both of them usually need to make changes to their finances, and it is rare that both of them will continue using the same financial planner. If you can develop a great relationship with a divorce attorney, you could have a lot of business coming your way.

Bereavement counselors: When someone loses a spouse, they have many decisions to make regarding the future. If the spouse who died was the one who handled most of the investments, it is likely the surviving spouse will make a change and find their own advisor to help them move forward.

Insurance agents: Insurance agents are already talking to their clients about risk, financial security, and the future. It is natural that their clients will also ask about investments and portfolios. Since most insurance agents can't help them in these matters, they need a valued partner like you to refer to their clients.

Business attorneys: Business attorneys help a lot of entrepreneurs start businesses, as well as help companies dissolve partnerships and figure out financial arrangements. Often, the individuals involved in the business need help with their own finances, so this can be an ideal referral source for you.

Centers of influence: Centers of influence are similar to referral partners, but they are better connected. Do you have a friend or colleague who seems to know everyone in town? If so, you've just identified a center of influence. It really doesn't matter what industry they are in. Centers of influence have pull with a wide range of people and can often introduce you to those in the community who can help your business. It is smart to cultivate a relationship with at least a couple of these individuals by taking them to lunch on a monthly basis or meeting up for coffee or a round of golf. If you can get "in" with a strong center of influence, it can benefit your business enormously.

Developing mentors: I am always expounding on the importance of having mentors. They can help your business in myriad ways because they have already been in your shoes. I suggest developing at least five or more mentoring relationships with individuals who are at various stages in their businesses. A few should be in the financial industry, but some can be in other areas of business as well. The important thing is that they have been in the trenches and are willing to give you advice to help you become a better business owner.

Will mentors help you bring in clients? They might not do so directly as a referral partner would, but they will undoubtedly help you take your business to the next level. Not only can they tell you how they personally grow their own business and increase their clients' numbers, but they can also give you insight into what didn't work for them and how you can avoid similar pitfalls.

WEBSITE

Entrepreneurs often struggle with their online presence, especially if they have spent their careers working for large firms that handle all of this for them. However, now that you are self-employed, it is vital that you are represented professionally when clients or prospects search for you online. Take these steps to build your own business website.

Logo: A memorable and professional-looking logo is not only important for your website, it is crucial to your overall brand. This logo will appear on all your collateral marketing materials, your website, and on your envelopes and correspondence.

You may want to sketch out some options for your logo, but I encourage you to employ a professional graphic designer. I've seen too many entrepreneurs hurt themselves by designing their own logo that ends up looking lackluster. If, however, you have a low budget, you can create your own logo for $5 on Fiverr, an online marketplace for freelance services.

Domain: Every website needs a domain name, which is your website's address. To get a domain name, you simply need to buy and secure it. But wait—sometimes it is not that easy. If the name of your business is common, the domain name you desire could already be taken, or it could be very expensive. It makes sense to investigate available domains before you name your company. However, if you have already chosen a name, you may find that you need to secure a domain name slightly different than your actual business name.

For example, if you named your business, Next Generation Financial, you may have to choose a domain such as NxtGenFin. com or Next-Generation-Fin.com if NextGenerationFinancial. com is already taken. If the name of your domain is not exactly the same as the name of your company, don't worry. When you properly market your site and put in plenty of SEO (Search Engine Optimization) work, prospects will have no problems finding your site.

Working with a professional website company: Depending on where you are at in your professional journey, you may want to build your own website to save costs, or you may want to outsource the work to maximize results and save time. Unless you have a background in web design or IT, I almost always recommend that you work with professionals to develop your brand and website and to handle ongoing maintenance on your site. Although you will pay more upfront costs when you use a professional website company, it will save you time and money in the long run.

However, if you have recently graduated from college and are new to the industry, you likely do not have a large budget to do so. You can create a website on your own using Wix, a web development platform that allows users to create their own website using online drag and drop tools. These sites are easy to create, tweak, manage, and blog from. Wix is incredibly user-friendly.

If you are established in the industry, then you can surely hire a company to build your website, which will free up your time and energy to meet more clients and develop deeper relationships in the field. You also could consider only outsourcing part of the work, seeking a designer to help specifically with logos or landing pages, for example.

I highly encourage the entrepreneurs I mentor to work with a professional website company once they have the budget to do so. The money you'll spend on these services will be well worth it. It is not your area of expertise to design, host, and update a website. Your area of expertise is building relationships with clients and advising them along their path to financial wellness. The more time you take away from your talent to tend to areas where you lack talent, the more it will hurt your business.

Lastly, your website needs to be secure. If any of your clients send you messages or make comments on your website that reveal private information, you could get into serious trouble. You also want to be sure your website is safe against cyber criminals who can do untold damage to your website and business. Put forth great effort to ensure your website is safe and secure.

EMAIL AND TEXTS

Are your emails secure? Not only do you need to protect your inbox against unauthorized use, you also need to have an encryption system so your emails cannot be hacked. Archiving solutions software keep your emails private and encrypted preventing hackers from gaining access to them.

Speaking of archiving, many advisors communicate with clients via text. While this is handy, it can also breach security. First of all, you should never send private information via text—like social security or account numbers, account details, or anything else that could be used negatively against your clients in the future. Secondly, you cannot always control what your clients text you. This is why it is important to have a text archiving service on your phone that stores your texts in a secure manner.

BUSINESS CARDS AND COLLATERAL

Having a professional image is vital to your business. If you get involved in networking groups, meet with referral partners, or develop strong ties to community organizations, you will pass out a lot of business cards or marketing materials such as pens or notepads to keep you top-of-mind with your prospects. Consider these steps to develop a positive professional image.

Work with a professional designer: Can you slap your logo on a business card template and call it good? Of course you can, but it will show. It is well worth it to work with a professional designer (ideally the same one who designed your logo) to design quality business cards that make a good impression.

Think outside the box: Your competitors will also hand out collateral material, and you don't want yours to get lost in the shuffle. So get creative with what you hand out! There are hundreds of great products you can brand with your logo. I suggest working with a promotional products representative who can listen to your needs and make suggestions for unique items that will make you stand out in the crowd.

Don't over-order: The last thing you want is to pay for boxes of items you can't give away. Although you'll pay a little more per item, order reasonable quantities of your collateral marketing products. This allows you to be flexible and change up the types of products you offer so that you can give away new and fresh items.

SOCIAL MEDIA

Social media is an important part of your marketing strategy, especially if you are trying to drive traffic to your website, but it can be tricky for new entrepreneurial advisors. Those who have worked for large firms may be reluctant to participate in social media because many of those firms have strict compliance departments that prevent their advisors from posting much of anything. Fortunately, these rules lighten up a lot when you go out on your own.

Many new advisors are also overwhelmed by frequent algorithm changes, the amount of time it takes to keep a robust social media presence, and, of course, those compliance requirements. So start simple. Establish social media accounts for your business on Facebook, Instagram, and Twitter, and start posting to them regularly to gain visibility in the market.

Whether you use social media in your personal life or not, understand that it is a powerful tool for your new business. You need it. If you don't care for social media or don't have time to utilize it properly, consider hiring someone to do it for you. This is especially true for older advisors who have never gotten into the social media world. Younger generations grew up with this stuff and are proficient in harnessing its power. You will be able to get a lot more out of your social media presence by hiring a part-time college student than you would be trying to figure it out for yourself. As your business grows, this position can transition into a full-time marketing role.

Your goal with social media is not to gain clients (although that will happen if you use it properly). Your goal is to give value. That comes in the form of sharing helpful articles and resources, providing information your followers would find valuable, and setting up yourself as a resource—not as a salesperson. We encourage those we work with to adhere to an 80/20 rule. Eighty percent of what you post shouldn't be about you or your company at all. This should be information that offers value to the client. Only twenty percent of your posts should even mention you or what you do. By adhering to this guideline, you ensure your audience is engaged and informed, and you are top-of-mind when they need a quality advisor.

Here is a list of social media guidelines to follow as you ramp up your online presence.

1. **Create a social media policy:** Your social media policy should be written and kept on file. The policy needs to specify what can and cannot be communicated on social media. It should also include which social media channels the firm can post to.

2. **DO NOT use client testimonials:** The testimonial rule is Rule 206(4)-1(a)(1) of the Investment Advisors Act of 1940, and it applies to social media.

3. **Archive:** Advisors must archive all social media posts and advertisements across all platforms.

4. **LinkedIn:** Do not allow endorsements on LinkedIn.

5. **Do not make promises:** Treat social media like everyday conversations. Do not allow misleading information such as guarantees or promised investment returns. Do not post comments that could be misleading.

6. **Review:** Make sure all posts are reviewed and approved for regulatory compliance.

7. **Use social media to educate your prospects and**

clients: Social media is a great tool to demonstrate your value. Instead of selling online, use it to teach your audience.

8. **Declaration:** Put in place a procedure or training to notify employees that social media accounts are owned by the firm.

9. **Do not cross channels:** Enforce a policy that states employees can't use their own social media accounts for business related communication if it isn't supervised by the firm.

10. **Audit:** An audit procedure will ensure all social media channels and employees are compliant.

ADVANCED MARKETING OPTIONS

Once you are ready, you can take your online marketing efforts to the next level by focusing on SEO and blogging, two marketing plans that go hand-in-hand.

SEO: Search Engine Optimization, is the process of organically affecting your website's online visibility. This can maximize your website's search engine's results. There are a number of different components to SEO. If you work with a professional website company, they will ensure your website copy has correct keywords and is fully SEO-optimized. If you have created your own website, be sure to include plenty of keywords and phrases such as "financial advisor in (city where your office is)," "independent financial advisor," "investment options in (city)," etc. This will increase your rankings, so you will show up higher in searches when your prospects are looking online for a new advisor.

Blogging: A big part of SEO is having fresh content regularly on your website. That's where your blog comes in. If you are frequently (once a week) publishing blogs that are informative for readers and include keywords, you can easily boost your SEO and help people find you online. If you're not a writer, I encourage you to hire a ghostwriter or freelancer for your blogs. You give them the information they need via written notes, recordings, or in-person meetings, and then edit the work to ensure it is in your voice and tone. If you do not have experience writing, don't spend a day agonizing over a post that a professional writer can knock out in a half hour. Once again, utilize professional help so you can spend your time honing your strengths and building relationships.

Marketing your business may feel like a lot of work, but you can do this! If you focus on a good website, optimize your SEO, and develop a consistent blogging and social media strategy, you will be well ahead of many of your competitors.

CONCLUSION

CONCLUSION

I desire you to be a successful entrepreneur in this great world of financial planning, and I hope I have empowered you to begin. This book implies that your journey is a partnership. You are not alone! However you decide to become an advice-based financial planner, I am here for you along the way. I am with you on this journey, and I know you can be successful. I am excited for you! I am filled with gratitude to be able to mentor and guide another successful financial advisor into this busy world. We need you!

This book is just the beginning of our partnership. I invite you now to participate in our online courses at True Measure, seek one-on-one mentorship available at our website, and grow your business with the help of our free and evolving resources online and robust social media content. We are prepared to accompany you to become a seven-figure, advice-based business owner.

It truly is an honor to advise families and positively influence their financial well-being, and I look forward to you experiencing the gratification of being an influential and successful financial advisor.

ABOUT THE AUTHOR

ABOUT THE AUTHOR

Patrick Tucker, owner of True Measure, has over 20 years of experience in the financial services industry and founded True Measure Wealth Management to help people explore the wisdom of true wealth. Patrick also founded True Measure Advisors to teach other Financial Planning Advisors how to attain the same level of entrepreneurial freedom and fulfillment as he has.

He is dedicated to lifelong learning himself and helps revive other's curiosity for learning as well. He continues to put his clients first and strongly opposes the side of the financial industry that focuses on sales.

Patrick was born and raised in Minnesota. He has been happily married to his wife, Sue, for 27 years and together they are the proud parents of six sons. Patrick is a passionate nutrition and fitness nerd who enjoys the outdoors and loves spending time with family, reading, cooking, and forever learning new things.

ABOUT THE COMPANY

ABOUT THE COMPANY

When Patrick left his job with a big bank in 2001, he knew he wanted to create an independent financial advisory business that provided value and direction. However, it wasn't until he lost his biggest account due to financial sales that he realized his true vision. That one loss showed him that his calling was to become a financial caregiver for his clients—not a financial products salesperson.

Patrick vowed to never again accept a commission on any financial product he recommended and felt called to help other advisors realize their "true measure" through advice-based planning. He built True Measure on this basis and continues to study investor behavior and the soft sciences to be a resource to his clients and to financial advisors he coaches. With Patrick's wealth of knowledge, he has the ability to lead his clients and advisor students down a path of financial success and personal fulfillment that is unprecedented in the industry.